The Truth (& Myths) about Disasters

by L. A. Peacock

illustrated by Jon Davis

Scholastic Inc.

For Joan, Cathy, and Carolyn — L.A.F.

Photographs ©: 5: edella/Thinkstock; 8: U.S. Geological Survey; 16: Chicago History Museum/Getty Images; 20: NOAA; 26: Nian Yifeng/ZUMApress/Newscom; 28, 31, 33, 37: Library of Congress; 41: Everett Collection Historical/Alamy Images; 43: Photo Researchers, Inc./Science Source; 47: National Archives; 51: U.S. Department of Health and Human Services; 52: Rich Legg/Thinkstock; 54: Ringo Chiu/ZUMAPRESS/Newscom; 56: George E. Marsh Album/NOAA; 61: John McColgan/USDA Forest Service; 63: Mike McMillan/Spotfire Images; 65: Petty Officer 2nd Class Tom Sperduto/U.S. Coast Guard; 67: Chris Corder UPI Photo Service/Newscom; 72: Kyodo News/Newscom; 75: NOAA; 77: Vincent Laforet/ AP Images; 79: Jocelyn Augustino/FEMA; 80: Aneese/Thinkstock; 81: U.S. Coast Guard; 83: Joe Raedle/Thinkstock; 84: AP Images; 88: Comstock/Thinkstock; 89: Mike Hollingshead/Solent News/AP Images; 91: Facethewind/Thinkstock.

ISBN 978-0-545-70565-3

12 11 10 9 8 7 6 5 4   16 17 18 19/0
Printed in the U.S.A.   40

First edition, October 2014

Contents

Chapter 1
Volcanoes: Mount Vesuvius, August 24, 79 A.D.; Mount St. Helens, May 18, 1980

What surprised the citizens of Pompeii on August 24, 79 AD?

Nearby Mount Vesuvius blew its top! It was a volcano. Thick clouds of fire and dust buried the Roman town. About two thousand people were trapped in ten feet of ash. Over time, the ash around the bodies hardened, leaving the shapes of the dead people behind.

Why is Pompeii a famous museum now?

Today we can walk through the streets of the town and see how the early Romans lived. Loaves of bread are still in bakers' ovens. Dinner tables are set with fruit, eggs, and vegetables. There is even a sick boy in bed with a plate of chicken next to him.

Didn't the people of Pompeii know about the volcano?

Yes, they knew, but they thought the mountain was asleep. The last eruption was three hundred years earlier. Some people felt **tremors,** or shaking in the earth. That morning, dogs barked wildly and birds flew away. But people ignored these warning signs from nature.

THE NAME VOLCANO COMES FROM VULCAN.

THAT'S THE ANCIENT ROMAN GOD OF FIRE.

TRUTH or MYTH?

Vesuvius is the world's most visited volcano.
TRUTH! Even today, tourists climb up to look into the steaming crater. It's the only active volcano in mainland Europe.

What's a volcano?

It's an opening in the Earth's crust. Hot molten rock, or **magma**, is deep inside the earth. Sometimes the magma mixes with hot gases and moves upward. It punches through the crust and flows out as **lava**. As the top of the mountain becomes unplugged, the volcano explodes.

ASH AND ROCKS

FOUNTAINS OF LAVA

CENTRAL OPENING

MAGMA

Are there volcanoes under the sea?

Yes. In fact, there are more eruptions under the ocean than on land. Over time, lava and ash from some of these undersea volcanoes can pile up and create new islands.

Are there any volcanoes in the U.S.?

Yes. Alaska has the most volcanoes.

When did Washington State's Mount St. Helens erupt?

On May 18, 1980, this volcano blew its cap off. Before the blast, the mountain was 9,677 feet tall. Now, it's 8,364 feet. The eruption left a horseshoe-shaped **crater** at the top. The energy released was the same as five hundred atom bombs.

How bad was the blast on Mount St. Helens?

It was the worst in U.S. history. Almost sixty people died. Volcanic ash traveled about fifteen miles into the air, then spread across the country to the eastern states and to countries around the world. Ash from the explosion spread over an area of twenty thousand square miles.

Was there a lava flow?

Yes. The lava flow traveled sixteen miles and killed all the trees in its path.

Was there other the damage in the area?

More than 200 houses, 27 bridges, 15 miles of rail lines, and 185 miles of highway were destroyed.

What about wildlife?

Tens of millions of fish, birds, and animals were killed in the blast.

How many animals were killed at Mount St. Helens?

A lot, including about:

- 200 black bears
- 300 bobcats
- 5,200 elk
- 1,400 coyotes
- 11,000 hares
- 15 mountain lions

How long will it take for trees and plants to return?

Scientists estimate it will take more than two hundred years to regrow the forest around Mount St. Helens.

TRUTH or MYTH?

Wild weather and earthquakes cause the worst disasters.

MYTH! The deadliest disasters are caused by bacteria, viruses, and other tiny **organisms**. These germs attack the body through open cuts, the air we breathe, the food we eat, and the water we drink. Each year, more than thirteen million people throughout the world die from diseases such as malaria, cholera, and AIDS.

For thousands of years, what disease made the most people sick?

Smallpox. It traveled easily from person to person in a sneeze or a cough. Blisters, or sores filled with pus, covered the bodies of infected people. One in three people with the disease died.

YOU GET SMALLPOX FROM PEOPLE WHO CARRY THE VIRUS AND FROM OBJECTS THEY TOUCHED.

Was there any smallpox in North America before the 1600s?

No, the disease was brought to the New World by the early explorers, slaves, and settlers from Europe, Asia, and Africa.

More than twenty million Native Americans died of smallpox. That's 95 percent of the total **population**!

Did the Pilgrims find smallpox when they landed in Plymouth, Massachusetts, in 1620?

No, but they found the bones of dead Indians. The Patuxent people, who used to live there, had probably died from smallpox.

How did inoculation work?

A needle or sharp toothpick was used to take some pus from a sore on an infected person. Then, a healthy person was scratched on the arm with the virus. The person might be sick for a few days. After that, the person was **immune**, or protected, from the disease. But one in fifty died.

How did Colonial Americans learn about inoculation?

Cotton Mather, a Boston clergyman, found out about the procedure from his African slave. His son and 280 others were **inoculated** in the next smallpox epidemic of 1721. Soon, people in other cities wanted to get inoculated.

"VACCINE" MEANS "OBTAINED FROM A COW" IN LATIN.

How did milkmaids in England help bring an end to smallpox?

In 1778, British country doctor Edward Jenner noticed that most milkmaids had clear, smooth skin. They almost never got smallpox. Sometimes they got a mild case of cowpox from milking cows. Jenner took cowpox virus from cows and developed a vaccine. Once vaccinated with cowpox, people might get headaches and chills, but they became immune to smallpox, a much more dangerous disease.

What president brought vaccination to the American West?

Thomas Jefferson. He sent supplies of the vaccine with explorers Lewis and Clark. But most Indians were afraid of the strange needles and refused. Many tribes in the Great Plains and the Pacific Northwest continued to die in great numbers from smallpox.

When was the last known case of smallpox?

In 1977. The vaccine had been given to millions around the world. Smallpox has become the only natural disease to be totally eliminated.

Does the smallpox virus still exist?

Yes, but only for study by scientists, not in any living person. Frozen samples of the virus are kept in Atlanta, Georgia, and in Koltsovo, Russia.

Chapter 3
Great Chicago Fire: October 8, 1871

How bad was the fire that swept through Chicago in 1871?

It was so bad that the city almost burned to the ground. At the time, there were almost sixty thousand buildings. But two-thirds were made of wood. Most had tar or shingle roofs, which caught fire easily. It was a city waiting to burn.

How much was the damage?

More than three hundred people died and 17,500 buildings were destroyed. A hundred thousand people were left homeless. Some people threw all their belongings into wagons. Even some of these caught fire as their owners tried to flee the flames.

Mrs. O'Leary's milk cow started the fire.

MYTH! The famous story that her cow kicked over a kerosene lantern and set the fire is a local legend. No one knows the real cause of the fire, but it may have started in the O'Leary barn.

Who saw flames in the barn?

It wasn't the O'Leary family. They were fast asleep. A neighbor, Daniel "Peg Leg" Sullivan, saw the blaze first.

WHY WAS HE CALLED THAT?

SULLIVAN HAD A WOODEN LEG.

What did Peg Leg Sullivan do?

He yelled "Fire! Fire! Fire!" and rushed into the burning building. Peg Leg fell. His wooden leg got stuck between two boards and came off. He hopped toward the door, carrying a calf to safety.

How close to the O'Leary barn was the nearest fire hydrant?

Eleven blocks away. At first, the *wrong* fire-alarm box was struck. Fire engines were sent on a wild-goose chase. They ended up at a place one mile from the fire.

What famous document was destroyed in the fire?

President Abraham Lincoln's draft of the Emancipation Proclamation. It was lost when Chicago's Historical Society building burned to the ground.

When did the fire end?

At eleven o'clock Monday night. When it started to rain, the fire finally cooled off. The raging fire had swept through 2,100 acres in thirty-one hours.

What happened to the O'Leary house and barn?

Surprisingly, they were not destroyed by the fire, even though everything around them burned. In 1956, the old buildings were finally torn down. A school to train Chicago firefighters was built on the site.

How did Chicago rebuild after the Great Fire?

The modern skyscraper was born. Insurance companies didn't want to insure wooden buildings. In 1885, William Le Baron Jenney figured out how to use steel, a new material, to frame and hold up big concrete buildings. Skyscrapers changed city life. Now thousands of people could live and work in smaller spaces.

Chapter 4
Great Blizzard of 1888

When did the Great Blizzard of 1888 start?

Which one? There were *two* of them! The first was between January 12 and 14 and occurred in the Great Plains, then moved across the Midwest. More than 235 people lost their lives. A second storm struck the Northeast on March 11.

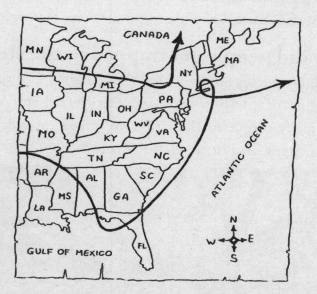

How bad was the Northeast storm?

It was the worst on record for the region. Snowfalls often reached up to fifty-five inches. Around four hundred people died, half in New York City.

What else besides snow was blowing around?

Lots of garbage. Trash, newspapers, and other litter filled the streets. The city's sixty thousand horses added five hundred thousand pounds of their own manure. In the storm, all this smelly stuff hardened and blew into the faces of people.

How did people get trapped in the storm?

Ice built up quickly on the streets. The trains stopped running. Heavy gusts of wind blew snow and sleet everywhere. Without trains, many people in the city were forced to walk in the blizzard. Some died frozen in the streets.

Why did people try to walk in the storm?

They were afraid of losing their jobs. An economic depression was going on, so jobs were hard to get. Many workers battled the storm to get to their factories and offices.

NEW YORK LOST THREE MILLION DOLLARS IN BUSINESS.

LATER, THE CITY BUILT THE UNDERGROUND SUBWAY SYSTEM.

LAWS AGAINST LITTERING WERE PASSED, TOO.

Did ten-year old Rufus Billings get to school?

Yes. He put on his boots and fought the snow to reach his school in Brooklyn. When he got there, he found classmates but no teachers. The door was locked. The kids waited for an hour. Finally, the principal arrived, only to send them home!

Was there enough food?

No. The blizzard lasted for three days. People in **tenements** didn't have refrigerators. They usually bought food on the day they cooked. After the storm, food prices skyrocketed. The cost of chickens jumped from seven cents to twenty-five cents, and eggs from twenty-five cents to forty cents a dozen. And some people in 1888 earned only three dollars a week!

Where did poor people spend the night?

The storm was hardest on the poor. Thousands lived in tenements. Often, seven families crowded inside one apartment. Less lucky were the city's sixty thousand homeless people, about fifteen thousand of them were children. During the blizzard, most soup kitchens and church basements filled quickly. Some people spent the night in cardboard boxes over steam grates on sidewalks.

How was the snow cleared from train tracks?

By hand. The railroad hired a thousand **immigrants** to shovel the snow in the roaring blizzard.

SHOVELING SNOW PAID $1.20 FOR A TEN-HOUR DAY.

How else can snow kill people?

One way is by an avalanche. Each year, about one hundred people die in the European Alps. When snow builds up on the side of a mountain, a giant piece can break off and sweep down. A strong wind, a temperature change, or an earthquake—even a skier—can set off an avalanche.

Can you survive an avalanche?

One in twenty people do. Those buried in snow need to be rescued in fifteen minutes before they run out of air or freeze to death.

Rescue workers find people trapped in the snow by using . . .
a) sound detectors
b) heat detectors
c) *radar*
d) long rods or poles

All of the above. Specially trained dogs are used, too.

What causes snow to have a rosy color?

Pink snow fell on Durango, Colorado, on January 9, 1932. *Red* snow coated the Alps on October 14, 1775, and over Italy and Switzerland on February 3–4, 1852. The snow in Europe was colored by dust in the **atmosphere** carried there by winds from the Sahara desert.

What about other colors?

Black and *blue* snow was reported in New York State in April 1889. The snow contained soil made up of very fine dirt and vegetable mold. *Yellow* snow fell on Bethlehem, Pennsylvania, on March 16, 1879. It was filled with pollen from pine trees in bloom in states to the south.

Do stories about floods go all the way back to the Bible?

Yes, Noah's ark. According to the Bible, this big boat floated on a flood caused by forty days of heavy rain. Noah's family and animals stayed on the ark for one year until the waters dried up.

TRUTH or MYTH?

Many early civilizations began on the floodplains of mighty rivers.

TRUTH! The ancient Egyptians, for example, settled on the fertile land where the Nile River flows into the sea. The people relied on the river flooding each year to grow their crops

Why do so many people die in floods?

About half of the world's population lives close to rivers or along coastlines.

Why do serious floods always happen in countries like the Netherlands and Bangladesh?

Because most of these lands are below sea level. The Dutch started to build dikes, or walls, to hold back the sea in the eleventh century. But storms and high tides still brought floods. More than four hundred thousand Dutch people drowned in 1530. In Bangladesh, each year the **monsoons** trigger floods. In 1997–98, more than half of the country was underwater. Twenty-five million people lost their homes.

What are some of the natural causes of flooding?

a) hurricanes

b) tsunamis

c) heavy rainfall

d) storm **surges**

e) avalanches

The answers are *a*, *b*, *c*, and *d*. Almost half of the victims of all natural disasters die from floods. Some die from drowning; others from the effects of floods, such as diseases and starvation.

What happens during times of heavy rainfall?

The ground becomes **saturated** and can't absorb any more water. The extra rainwater flows into rivers and lakes. Dams can't hold back the rising water. They give way, flooding nearby towns.

How did more than two thousand people die in Johnstown, Pennsylvania, on May 31, 1889?

They drowned in less than ten minutes. One hundred days of rain and melting snow caused the local river waters to rise quickly. Fourteen miles upriver, a dirt dam burst. It was holding back a man-made lake. Four billion gallons of water gushed toward Johnstown. Trees and houses in its path were swept away.

What did people do when they saw the raging floodwaters?

Some families climbed on top of roofs, but they were swept along as buildings disappeared. When the floodwater reached Johnstown, it was filled with destroyed trees and homes. Even one hundred-ton train cars looked like toys riding the waves.

What happened to the Waters family?

Some of them hung on to the attic beams of their new house. But Mrs. Waters fell off the roof. She kept her head above the flood and held her baby girl out of the water.

How did six-year-old Gertrude Quinn Slattery get saved?

She was carried along the water on a wet, muddy mattress. A roof with twenty people floated toward her. Gertrude shouted for help. A man jumped into the water and climbed onto her mattress. Together, they floated downstream. Later, the man threw Gertrude fifteen feet from the mattress into the arms of rescuers.

How deadly was the Johnstown flood?

Nearly four hundred children drowned. Some bodies of flood victims were found as far away as Cincinnati, Ohio.

Who helped in the rescue effort?

Ten thousand workers were hired to clean up the wreckage. Almost four million dollars of relief money was collected. Schoolchildren sent in nickels and dimes. Entertainer Buffalo Bill Cody staged a Wild West show as a fund-raiser. In 1926, the story of the disaster was made into a Hollywood silent film.

Who else came to help?

Clara Barton arrived on the scene with her new organization, the American Red Cross. She stayed for five months, bringing food and shelter to the homeless.

What event rocked one of America's great cities in 1906?

An earthquake. Within a few seconds, most of San Francisco was reduced to rubble. The shaking sent out shock waves more than seven thousand miles per hour across three hundred miles of land, with San Francisco at the **epicenter**.

Why did San Francisco grow so fast after 1848?

Gold was discovered in the California hills. The next year, people from China and New York came in ships. Farmers and factory workers crossed the Rockies to seek their fortune. Most miners failed to find gold. Instead, these "forty-niners" crowded into San Francisco to look for work. Many started new businesses.

Did Levi Strauss make his fortune in the gold rush?

Yes, but not from mining. He brought his "blue canvas" cloth from New York and started making clothes for miners. His sturdy blue jeans quickly became a best seller.

YOUR DISASTERS I.Q.

What new words and terms came from the gold rush?

a) bonanza

b) to strike it rich

c) pay dirt

d) pan out

All of the above. We still use these expressions today.

What did the earthquake feel like?

Most people were asleep. At 5:12 a.m., the **plates** below San Francisco made a major shift. The first tremor hit. Twenty-five seconds later, the earth shook again for almost sixty seconds. Buildings crumbled and streets caved in. Fires started as fireplaces collapsed and wires were cut. Gas pipes burst. By noon, a wall of fire spread out over a mile and a half. Soon, half the city was ablaze.

How did the survivors get out?

Thousands of citizens walked around the fire. They pushed toy wagons and baby carriages filled with their belongings. Some headed for the beaches. Others crowded into railcars. More than 225,000 were carried away in trains. Another twenty thousand boarded the U.S.S. *Chicago* and other ships to escape the burning city by sea.

Did the government help?

Yes. Thousands of soldiers helped **evacuate** the city. The governor sent food and medical supplies. Congress dispatched relief trains. President Teddy Roosevelt ordered warships to pump water and put out the fires.

How did they finally put out the fires?

Dynamite was used to blast twenty-two blocks of Van Ness Avenue. This created a firebreak to hold back the flames and stop the fire from spreading.

How long did the fire burn?

For three days. About 490 city blocks were destroyed. Almost thirty thousand buildings were lost, including thirty-one schools. More than one hundred thousand people camped outside and cooked in the streets.

What did health officials do?

They knew that the disease was spread by fleas on infected rats. The officials were clever, so they offered to pay money to citizens for dead rats. In all, two million rats were poisoned and only seventy-seven people died from plague.

How was the rubbish in the streets cleaned up?

There were piles of bricks everywhere. Thirty-one million of them. And everyone helped pick them up. New rail tracks were laid throughout the city. Fifteen thousand loads carried away the debris and dumped it into the bay. Today, San Francisco's Marina District stands on this landfill.

How many people live in the San Francisco Bay Area today?

About eight million people. That's eight times more than in 1906.

Will there be another earthquake?

Probably. Every year, ten thousand earthquakes shake California. Most are minor and cause no damage. Since 1906, the San Andreas Fault has been moving an inch and a half a year, or sixteen feet. Scientists check their equipment daily for shock waves. But nobody knows when or where the next big quake will occur.

THE 1906 QUAKE MEASURED ABOUT 7.9 ON THE RICHTER SCALE.

THE HIGHEST LEVEL IS TEN!

Can the city survive another big quake?

City officials think so. There are new building codes. Since 1972, no schools, hospitals, power plants, or homes can be built near fault lines. Architects today use new materials and methods that make buildings and bridges earthquake-proof.

Chapter 7
Triangle Shirtwaist Fire: March 25, 1911

What's a sweatshop?

It's a place where many new immigrants worked long hours for low pay. Many left Europe and came to America in the early 1900s, searching for a better life.

What were sweatshops in 1911 like?

They were unhealthy and crowded. Most were located in big cities, such as New York. Sweatshops were often garment factories. The buildings were several stories high. On the floors, women worked at sewing machines on long tables. Young children worked, too, replacing empty spools of thread and sweeping floors. Dust was everywhere, flying off fabric and spinning spools.

What kinds of clothes were made in sweatshops?

Shirtwaists were popular. These were cotton blouses with puffed sleeves that women wore with long skirts.

TRUTH or MYTH?

It was against the law for children under fourteen to work in sweatshops.

TRUTH! But they often did. An eight-year-old boy might work long hours, seven days a week, and earn a dollar fifty. His mother could earn six dollars.

Why didn't they quit?

New immigrants needed money for the family to survive. There were too many of them and too few jobs. Workers started to protest and form **unions**. Some were beaten and put in jail. Names of people in unions were given to sweatshop owners. They were not hired.

What happened at the Triangle Shirtwaist Factory in New York City on September 7, 1909?

Hundreds of women and girls stopped their sewing machines and left the building. They demanded higher wages and safer working conditions. It was a bold action for women of the time.

Did the protest grow?

Yes. A general strike was held on November 22. More than twenty thousand workers from shirtwaist shops from all over New York City marched in the streets.

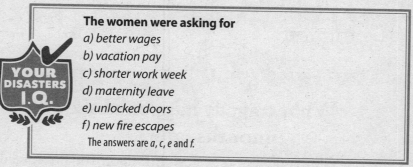

The women were asking for

a) better wages
b) vacation pay
c) shorter work week
d) maternity leave
e) unlocked doors
f) new fire escapes

The answers are *a, c, e* and *f*.

YOUR DISASTERS I.Q.

Did the strike work?

Yes, for some workers in sweatshops. But not for those in the Triangle Shirtwaist Factory.

Did the striking workers at the Triangle Factory keep their jobs?

No, they were replaced with *scabs*, or strikebreakers. The pay didn't get better. Doors were still locked to keep workers inside. Old fire escapes weren't replaced. The work space was crowded and dusty. The place was a fire hazard.

What tragedy happened six months later?

A fire started in a rag bin on the eighth floor. The fire spread quickly to fabric scraps, hanging paper patterns, and the wood floor.

Did anyone call a fire alarm?

Yes, workers called the ninth floor, but nobody answered. They threw pails of water on the flames. Finally, someone reached the boss on the tenth floor, who notified the fire department.

But for many it was too late. Women were trapped in the crowded rows of machines. Doors to stairways were locked. Many workers jumped from windows to their deaths.

What happened when the firemen arrived?

Three floors were already on fire. The firemen's ladders reached up only to the sixth floor. Workers on window ledges screamed for help. Elevators worked for a while. People on the top floors filled the cars. Some women even slid down ninety feet on the elevator cables. Others died in the elevator shaft.

Were the girls who jumped from eighty feet up saved?

No. Firemen below opened their nets. The women held hands and jumped. But they struck the nets at the same time. The firemen couldn't hold on, and the nets tore.

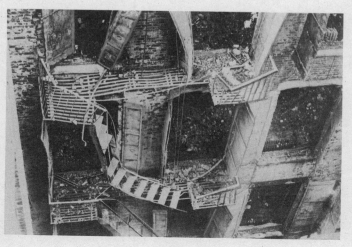

Did they get the fire out?

Yes. In less than thirty minutes, firemen put out the flames on the eighth floor. But 146 died, mostly women and young girls. Hundreds more were seriously burned. Seven workers who died were never identified.

THEY FOUND TWENTY FOUR WEDDING AND ENGAGEMENT RINGS IN THE ASHES.

Were there changes after the fire?

People were angry. New York City officials passed new rules. Fire alarms, fire drills, fire exits, fire escapes, and sprinklers were now required. They began to enforce child labor laws. In 1913, a fifty-four-hour work week became the law.

Chapter 8
Titanic: April 15, 1912

What was the biggest disaster in the history of Atlantic Ocean crossings?

The sinking of the *Titanic* on April 15, 1912. The ship set sail from Southampton, England, for New York City. That was its first and only voyage. After four days at sea, the ship struck an **iceberg** at night and sank.

Why was the *Titanic* called a "floating palace"?

It was built for luxury. The ship had nine decks and a crew of nine hundred to serve 1,300 passengers.

YOUR DISASTERS I.Q.

The *Titanic* had many first-class comforts, including
a) elevators
b) a swimming pool
c) air conditioning
d) a French café.
e) a gym

The answers are *a, b, d* and *e*. There was no air conditioning, but seventy-five fans provided some cool air.

Didn't the *Titanic* captain know about the dangerous icebergs in the Atlantic?

Yes, he got ice warnings from ships in the area all day. But the warning at 7:30 p.m. didn't reach him. He was at dinner.

What about the two crewmen on lookout?

They didn't have binoculars. They saw the iceberg when it got closer. The warning bell was struck at 11:40 p.m. The ship tried to turn, but it hit the iceberg thirty-seven seconds later. In less than ten seconds, the first officer pulled the lever to close the watertight doors below deck.

Why did people think the *Titanic* was unsinkable?

It was the largest passenger steamship in the world. Special airtight **compartments** were built. These small areas could be locked easily if water got in, to keep the ship from sinking.

What caused the damage?

The position of the ship when it struck the iceberg. There was a jolt, and some ice fell on deck. But the iceberg created big holes in the ship below the waterline. On the lower decks, water started gushing in. Five compartments filled up quickly. Water rose above this level and flooded the ship. The airtight compartments couldn't save the ship.

When did the crew know *Titanic* would sink?

Right away. Thomas Andrews, chief naval architect onboard, calculated that the ship would sink in an hour. It was "a mathematical certainty."

Were there enough lifeboats?

No. The ship's original plan called for thirty-two lifeboats. But the number was cut in half to make more space on deck for walking. There were only enough seats for about half of the 2,200 people on board.

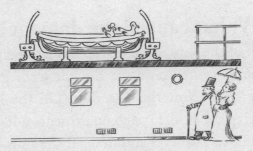

What about life jackets?

There were enough for everyone. But the water was freezing, about 28 degrees.

What happened while the ship was sinking?

People onboard panicked. First-class passengers ran to fill the lifeboats on the upper deck. In the rush to leave, many lifeboats pulled away with empty seats. If all seats had been filled, another five hundred people could have been saved.

TRUTH or MYTH?

Most of the first-class passengers survived.

TRUTH! Sixty-three percent were saved. Only 25 percent of third-class passengers and 42 percent in second class survived. Many who died were trapped below and drowned in the icy water.

Who was the first to answer *Titanic*'s distress signal?

The *Carpathia* was the nearest ship. She was fifty-eight miles away. It took three and a half hours to reach survivors.

TRUTH or MYTH?

The *Molly Brown* was one of the rescue ships.

MYTH! Mrs. James J. Brown was a Colorado millionaire in lifeboat 6. Molly gave her mink coat to an injured crew member. She showed the women how to row. They headed toward a ship and were rescued. We know her today as "Unsinkable Molly Brown."

What claims did the survivors put in for lost items?

Molly Brown claimed $500 for ancient artifacts bought for a Denver museum. One passenger claimed $50 for a set of bagpipes. A person made a claim for $100,000 for an oil painting. Another, $5,000 for an automobile.

Was the sunken *Titanic* ever found?

After more than seventy years. Robert D. Ballard, in a **submersible**, located the shipwreck in deep water, two and a half miles below the surface. Thousands of artifacts have been recovered, including a large soup bowl, silk socks, and leather bags. Even a glass jar filled with olives.

What was the worst illness in the history of the world?

A case of the flu! The **pandemic** influenza of 1918—an epidemic that spread so fast and killed so many—was twenty-five times more deadly than ordinary flu. Almost half of the world's population got sick. An estimated fifty million people died.

How did the flu affect soldiers fighting in World War I?

More than eleven thousand U.S. soldiers died of the flu while fighting in Europe. Another twenty-two thousand died in training camps in America. Soldiers were crowded together in tents and transport ships. They were easy targets for the disease.

TRUTH or MYTH?

The flu of 1918 was often called the Spanish flu.

TRUTH! When the epidemic reached Spain, eight million people caught the flu. In Madrid, a third of the population got sick. It got its name when first reports of the flu came from there

How did New York officials try to stop the spread of the disease?

If you coughed or sneezed in the street, you could pay a fine of $500 or go to jail for a year.

What warning did the *New York Times* give to young lovers?

To avoid the flu, the newspaper advised a man to kiss his girlfriend through a handkerchief.

How quickly did people die once they caught the flu bug?

Fast. One woman called to report her two roommates were dead and a third was ill. When the police arrived, they found *four* people dead!

Why did people wear gauze masks?

To protect from flu germs. But using masks did no good. The microscopic virus passed easily through the thin material.

What were some homemade remedies people used to fight the flu?

a) eat raw onions
b) tie cucumber slices to shoes
c) wear bags of insect repellant
d) remove toenails and teeth
e) carry potatoes in pockets
All of the above.

Why didn't doctors develop a flu vaccine in 1918?

They tried, but the vaccines didn't work. These early vaccines didn't contain the flu virus. It wasn't until the 1930s, when the electron microscope was invented, that scientists could study viruses.

Have we had another flu that started in birds?

Yes. A new bird flu, H5N1, popped up in Asia in 1997. To stop the disease, millions of chickens were killed. But not before more than a hundred people died.

Can other animals get the flu?

We know pigs do. In China, millions of people, birds, and pigs all live close together. Pigs were responsible for the swine flu of 2009, causing 203,000 deaths worldwide.

What is becoming the biggest killer virus in history?

The global AIDS pandemic. It is caused by the virus known as HIV, which destroys the body's blood cells. Thirty-five million people around the world are infected with HIV.

Is there a cure for AIDS?

Not yet, but there are drugs that can slow the disease. Educating people about the disease can help prevent its spread.

Chapter 10
Dust Bowl of the 1930s

When does a *drought* start?

We're not sure. There is much less rain than usual. The soil dries out and plants begin to die. The water levels drop. Cracks appear in dried-out riverbeds and dry lakes. If a **drought** lasts a long time, animals and people might starve to death.

When was the worst drought in U.S. history?

During the heat waves of the 1930s, especially the summers of 1934 and 1936, and the fall of 1939. The drought covered an area of more than fifty million acres of the Great Plains and Midwest, from Texas to Canada and from Colorado to Illinois. It was also the time of the Great Depression. The banks had failed. One out of five workers had no job.

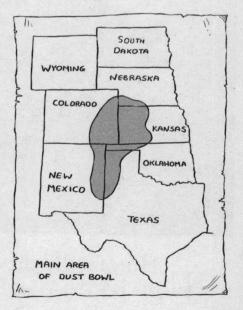

Why was this region called the Dust Bowl?

People mostly farmed here. When the drought struck, windstorms blew the topsoil into rolling clouds of dust.

How bad were the dust storms?

Some storms lasted for three days. The sun was blocked. Day was turned into night. In 1935, Texas had thirty-eight days in a row of dust.

How far did the dust blow?

Dust from the Great Plains reached America's East Coast. Some dirt even reached ships three hundred miles out in the Atlantic.

Where did the dust come from?

The farms of the Great Plains, mostly in Kansas, Oklahoma, Colorado, New Mexico, and Texas. The Great Plains Indians used to hunt **bison** on these grasslands. But the government broke treaties and moved the Indians off the land. Settlers came from the East. They replaced the bison with cows and sheep.

What happened to the grasslands on the Plains?

The farmers broke up the thick soil, or sod, into bricks to make houses. The grasslands were plowed for crops. Millions of acres now grew wheat. The rain cycle of the 1920s brought good crops.

What followed this rain cycle?

A drought cycle. The soil that was turned up by the plows began to blow away. Wells and ponds dried up. Cattle starved. People choked on the dust. Some died.

What was "Black Sunday"?

One of the worst storms. It happened on April 14. After many dust storms in the first half of April 1935, there was a break. It was a rare sunny day, but the air was still. Suddenly, blue sparks flashed along the wire fences. Peoples' hair stood on end. Rabbits headed south and birds screeched. A wall of dust came up from the north and blocked out the sun. Heavy dirt from the storm buried roads and caused houses to collapse. Some people went blind.

During the drought, which animals survived by the thousands?

a) cows

b) grasshoppers

c) rabbits

d) birds

The answers are *b* and *c*. Birds, snakes, and coyotes—their natural **predators**—had died. Insects ate whatever grass and crops were left. Rabbits multiplied so fast that farmers just shot them and left the meat to rot.

TRUTH or MYTH?

Most of the farmers stayed on their land.

TRUTH! But one in four left the Great Plains. They were called "Okies" even though most were not from Oklahoma. Thousands of these **migrants** headed west to California.

THERE WAS NO WORK OR FOOD.

MORE THAN THREE HUNDRED THOUSAND PEOPLE ABANDONED THEIR FARMS.

How did they travel?

Some jumped on trains. Others piled all of their belongings in old cars. They didn't have much money or food. They tried to find work along the way.

Did they find a better life in California?

No. They found mostly large, modern farms run like factories. Many got jobs as migrant workers, earning only seventy-five cents a day. Some looked for work in cities. They lived in shacks with no plumbing or electricity.

How did World War II help the Dust Bowlers?

When the U.S. went to war in 1941, it was a time of a rain cycle. Farmers were able to plant crops and get a good price for wheat. Those in California cities found jobs making ships and tanks for the military.

Chapter 11
Wildfires: Yellowstone National Park, 1988

How does the U.S. Fire Service manage wildfires?

Park firefighters track the weather, especially when summers are hot and dry. A bolt of lightning can spark a fire. Strong winds can fan the flames.

What direction do fires take?

The type of trees, weather, and geography of a region help predict a wildfire's likely movement.

How fast can the fires travel?

Up to speeds of 14 mph (miles per hour). That's faster than most people can run.

Can you always predict the direction of fires?

No. The 1988 fire in Yellowstone National Park burned nearly eight hundred thousand acres. It took only twenty-four hours for the fire to spread. The park service had estimated it would take two weeks to reach that far. They were wrong.

TRUTH or MYTH?

All wildfires are harmful.

MYTH! They are an important part of the life cycle of the forest. Wildfires burn off dead trees and plants and make the soil fertile again. But when they burn out of control, the fires can cause a lot of damage.

Are people in Southern California more afraid of earthquakes or wildfires?

Most probably fear wildfires. In 2004 alone, there were more than 5,500 fires spread across 168,000 acres.

PEOPLE CAUSE ABOUT HALF OF ALL WILDFIRES.

A LOT ARE CAUSED BY LIGHTNING.

How do airplanes and helicopters put out fires?

With special equipment that sucks up water from nearby lakes. Then the aircraft drop the water onto the fire. From the air, chemicals are sprayed to cool the flames and check the spread of the fire. Aircrafts also carry firefighters directly to the scene of the blaze.

Who are smoke jumpers?

These specially trained firefighters parachute into a wildfire. Their tools and pumps are dropped separately. Later, smoke jumpers have to hike out of the dangerous area carrying their equipment.

Which country has the most bushfires?

Australia, with an average of fifteen thousand bushfires each year.

How do the trees in the Australian bush grow back?

Most are eucalyptus trees. They are rich in natural oils, so they burn easily. When the trees are destroyed, they leave fertile ash in the soil. These trees also have fire-resistant seeds.

Chapter 12
Terrorist Attack: September 11, 2001

What event on September 11, 2001, shocked all Americans?

The worst terrorist attack in U.S. history. Two planes were hijacked from the Boston airport, one from Newark, New Jersey, and one from Washington, D.C. The two planes from Boston flew into and destroyed the World Trade Center towers in lower Manhattan. The third plane crashed into the Pentagon, in Washington, D.C., and the fourth, into an empty field in Pennsylvania. Its target was also in Washington, D.C.

How many people were killed?

Almost three thousand, including more than four hundred New York City firefighters and police officers who died when the Twin Towers collapsed.

Why was the World Trade Center chosen as a target?

The Twin Towers dominated the New York skyline of tall buildings. They were **symbols** to the world of Wall Street, the financial center of America.

THE TOWERS WERE ONE HUNDRED AND ELEVEN STORIES HIGH.

AND MADE OF TWO HUNDRED THOUSAND TONS OF STEEL.

What happened seventeen minutes after a plane hit the North Tower?

Another plane hit the South Tower. Everyone thought the first crash was an accident. News teams rushed to the scene. TV viewers around the world watched in horror as the second plane struck.

Why did so many people die?

The planes were filled with fuel, so the skyscrapers caught fire. People were trapped inside. Firefighters and police tried to rescue them from the burning buildings. But the steel structures collapsed, mostly from the heat of the flames.

How did the U.S. respond to the attacks?

President George W. Bush declared a War on Terror. He asked the nations of the world to help America in this fight. Later, the president sent American soldiers to Iraq and Afghanistan to find and destroy the terrorists.

Who planned and carried out the 9/11 attacks?

The terrorist group Al Qaeda and its leader, Osama bin Laden. Almost ten years later, bin Laden was found and killed in Pakistan by U.S. Navy SEALs. It was a surprise attack ordered by President Barack Obama.

The Empire State Building was the world's tallest until the Twin Towers were built.

TRUTH! The World Trade Center took seven years to build. It was officially opened on April 4, 1973.

How many people did it take to build the Towers?

About 3,500 workers a day.

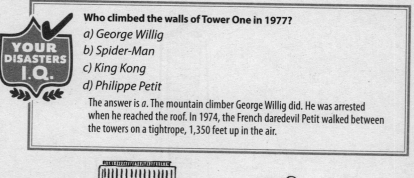

YOUR DISASTERS I.Q.

Who climbed the walls of Tower One in 1977?

a) George Willig

b) Spider-Man

c) King Kong

d) Philippe Petit

The answer is *a*. The mountain climber George Willig did. He was arrested when he reached the roof. In 1974, the French daredevil Petit walked between the towers on a tightrope, 1,350 feet up in the air.

Has New York rebuilt the World Trade Center?

Yes. At Ground Zero, the site of the former Twin Towers, there is a memorial to the victims of the 9/11 attack. A new skyscraper also stands there today—One World Trade Center. At 1,776 feet, it is the tallest building in the U.S.

Chapter 13
Indian Ocean Tsunami of 2004

TRUTH or MYTH?

A tsunami is a storm at sea.

MYTH! Winds don't make the deadly giant waves. Tsunamis are caused by undersea earthquakes.

What caused the deadly tsunami of 2004 in the Indian Ocean?

A huge earthquake on December 26 off the coast of Indonesia. The quake measured between 9.0 and 9.3 on the **Richter scale**. The seafloor moved upward about sixteen feet. This shift caused huge walls of water to roar toward coastlines in Asia and Africa.

How fast did the tsunami travel?

The water surges reached speeds of up to 500 mph.

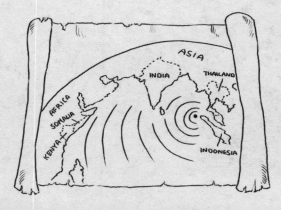

What happened when the tsunami hit Thailand's Phuket Island?

Waves up to thirty feet high rushed into the shore like a very fast tide. The water reached up to 1.2 miles inland. Many people lost their lives as the streets turned into rivers filled with debris.

Why did this tsunami kill three times more women than men?

In countries such as Indonesia, many women never learn how to swim. They have laws and **customs** that say women can only enter the water if they wear full clothing and head scarves.

How did ten-year-old Tilly Smith survive the tsunami?

On vacation in Thailand, Tilly was playing on the beach. She saw the great wave on the horizon. Tilly also noticed hundreds of tiny crabs crawling out of the water. She remembered a school lesson about the warning signs of tsunami. Tilly convinced her father to get the hotel to evacuate guests to higher ground. Because of Tilly's warning, her family and others were saved.

How did dolphins save lives?

Fishermen off the coast of Thailand saw dolphins jumping wildly, then turn and swim far out to sea. They knew that animals could sense unusual changes in nature. Quickly, the fishermen followed the dolphins into deeper water. They missed the full force of the tsunami.

Chapter 14
Hurricane Katrina: August 29, 2005

How is a hurricane born?

Strong winds from the earth's poles blow across the warm ocean waters. A storm grows as heat and water vapor are sucked up by the winds. Giant thunderclouds form. They start to spin, forming the hurricane. The storm can travel thousands of miles and last for weeks.

Where is the "eye" of a hurricane?

In the middle. The bands of thunderclouds spin around this calm, still center called the eye.

The Eye

Are there hurricanes in the Indian Ocean?

Yes, but they're called cyclones. In the Pacific, hurricanes are known as typhoons.

What forced a million Americans to leave their homes on August 29, 2005?

Hurricane Katrina. This major storm hit the southern coast of the U.S. Winds created a thirty-foot storm surge. The low-lying coastlines of Louisiana, Alabama, and Mississippi were flooded.

How powerful was Hurricane Katrina?

Winds of up to 175 mph made the storm a Category 5 when it crossed the warm waters of the Gulf and crashed into the coast. Nearly two thousand people died, and a million more were left homeless.

Why was New Orleans hit so hard?

Most of the city sits on land several feet below water level. It was built on mud carried by the Mississippi River as it flowed into the Gulf of Mexico.

Why has the city been rebuilt over and over again?

Because of the constant flooding. Over the years, high **levees**, or dikes, were built to protect New Orleans and hold back floodwaters. But the city was slowly sinking in the swampy soil. Today, there's not much land left to slow down the huge waves caused by hurricanes.

TRUTH or MYTH?

Hurricane Katrina slowed down when it hit New Orleans.
TRUTH! The winds slowed by mid-morning, but some of the levees failed. The real damage to the city was caused by the surge of water crashing through the broken walls.

How bad was the city flooded?

Eighty percent of the city was flooded. Many neighborhoods were under as much as twenty feet of water. It took three weeks to patch up the levees and pump the water out.

What happened when water flooded into New Orleans?

a) hundreds drowned

b) garbage filled the floodwaters

c) alligators, snakes, and rats swam into flooded houses

d) dead bodies floated in the waters

e) more than twenty-five thousand survivors filled the Superdome stadium

f) thousands of elderly and sick people were left without care

All of the above.

YOUR DISASTERS I.Q.

Why did it take so long to rescue people?

The government agencies didn't work well together. Some people used their boats and canoes to rescue survivors. Coast Guard helicopters pulled people from rooftops. It took five days to evacuate thousands of homeless people from the Superdome to other cities, many in Texas.

What happened after water was pumped out of the flooded city?

FEMA, the government relief agency, ordered more than one hundred thousand trailers and moved people into temporary housing. People all over the world donated money and supplies for the flood victims. Volunteers, some of them students on break from school, fixed damaged roofs and cleaned houses of debris and black mold. The U.S. Army Corps of Engineers designed and started to build new, stronger levees.

After Katrina, what was the second costliest weather disaster in American history?

Hurricane Sandy hit U.S. shores seven years later, in 2012. It caused at least 185 deaths and could cost up to $100 billion in damage on the East Coast.

Why was Sandy such a monster storm?

It covered such a wide area and hit the nation's largest city. The super storm caused huge floods in the New York area. It dropped three feet of snow in West Virginia and set off twenty-foot waves on the Great Lakes.

Chapter 15
Industrial Accidents: Oil Spills and Nuclear Meltdowns

What caused an explosion in the Gulf of Mexico on April 20, 2010?

An accident on the Deepwater Horizon oil rig. On the seafloor, pipes broke. **Crude** oil was released into the seawater for eighty-seven days. It was finally capped on July 15. By then an estimated 4.9 million barrels of oil had spilled into the Gulf. It was the largest oil spill in U.S. history.

ELEVEN OIL WORKERS WERE KILLED.

ANOTHER SEVENTEEN WERE INJURED IN THE BLAST.

Who was responsible for the blast?

A White House report put most of the blame on BP, British Petroleum, its owner and partners. They had poor safety systems and made bad decisions to cut costs. BP agreed to pay a record-setting $4.525 billion in fines.

Who else suffered from the spill?

Gulf Coast families and businesses sued to get money for lost property and wages. As of 2013, BP has paid out $42.4 billion to settle court cases.

TRUTH or MYTH?

It takes a long time to clean up an oil spill.

TRUTH! It can take years, often decades. The BP spill covered a huge region along the Gulf. **Contamination** spread to coastal areas, inland marshes, and river systems.

Was there damage to marine and wildlife habitats?

Yes, a lot. About thirty thousand rescue workers took part in the cleanup. They collected the spilled oil, cleaned the beaches, and rescued animals.

Do oil-contaminated animals die?

Most do. The oil is removed by washing a bird's body and wings in a mild dishwashing solution. Oily feathers prevent the bird from flying. Untreated birds often lose their **buoyancy**. They can't swim, so they drown.

Have there been serious spills from oil tankers?

Yes, the *Exxon Valdez* ran aground off the coast of Alaska in 1989. The tanker carried enough oil to fill 125 Olympic-sized swimming pools. Twelve years later, you could still find oil on nearby beaches.

What happened to the local animal population?

Countless salmon, herring, and other fish were destroyed. The spill also killed more than 250,000 seabirds, 2,800 sea otters, 250 bald eagles, 300 harbor seals, and 22 killer whales.

Have there been other kinds of industrial disasters?

Yes, in Ukraine, an accident occurred at the Soviet Union's Chernobyl **nuclear power** station on April 26, 1986. Fifty tons of deadly **radioactive** material escaped into the air. It was carried for miles, as far as Western Europe.

How much radiation went into the atmosphere?

Up to four hundred times the amount released from the atomic bomb dropped on the Japanese city of Hiroshima during World War II. The Soviet government ordered more than 150,000 people to evacuate the area around Chernobyl.

What happened to the people exposed to the radiation?

Thirty workers in the Chernobyl plant died. Some experts predicted many more would die later from cancers.

How did they cool down the nuclear reactor?

More than four thousand tons of lead, sand, and clay were dumped on the power plant by helicopters. Later, nitrogen was used to cool down the **reactor**.

What caused Japan's Fukushima Daiichi nuclear power plant to shut down?

A powerful earthquake and tsunami hit Japan on March 11, 2011. Several reactors at the plant were damaged and some radiation was released into the air. People living within twenty miles of the plant were evacuated.

Was there much damage?

Yes, to the economy. The Japanese people were anxious because of their World War II experience with the terrible power of atomic bombs. But those living near Fukushima have shown no bad effects of radiation. Radiation did contaminate the 2011 harvest. Crops in 2012 showed no sign of contamination.

Why are some children who live near Fukushima overweight today?

Schools nearby have stopped outside exercise. Students stay indoors, even though the risk from radiation is next to nothing.

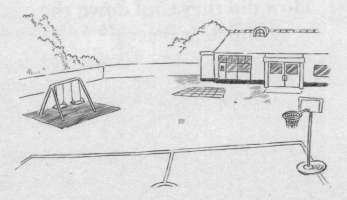

Chapter 16
Tornadoes: Moore, Oklahoma: May 20, 2013

How many tornadoes are there in the U.S. each year?

About a thousand. Most occur in the center of the U.S. known as Tornado Alley. This area includes the states of Kansas, Nebraska, Oklahoma, and Texas.

Why are there so many storms here?

It's where the warm, wet air from the Gulf of Mexico meets cold, dry air from the Rocky Mountains.

TRUTH or MYTH?

Most tornadoes occur in the U.S.

TRUTH! Eighty percent of the world"s tornadoes happen here. Bangladesh, Japan, South Africa, and the United Kingdom get them, too.

Are tornado winds worse than those of hurricanes?

Yes. Inside a tornado, wind speeds can be up to 300 mph. That's twice as fast as the worst hurricanes. But tornadoes travel only about six miles, and then die out.

TRUTH or MYTH?

Tornadoes take a long time to form.

MYTH! It takes anywhere from fifteen to ninety minutes for fluffy white clouds to turn into a deadly twister. A tornado lasts for only a few minutes.

How much damage?

A lot. Homes are flattened and trees snapped in two. People, cars, and cows have been lifted off the ground and dropped hundreds of feet away. Tornadoes passing over water can suck up fish and drop them later on land.

Who are the storm chasers?

These scientists follow a storm in trucks carrying Doppler radar equipment. They study storm clouds and look for a developing *vortex*. That's the air spinning inside, going up and down the tornado's column.

How does the National Weather Service monitor tornadoes?

With a lot of technology. They use information from 30 satellites, 122 Doppler radar systems, and 114 climate-data centers to forecast the weather. But scientists can't predict a tornado more than twenty-four hours in advance.

What happened at 2:40 p.m. on May 20, 2013?

Meteorologists knew that conditions were perfect for a monster tornado to strike Oklahoma. The Weather Service issued a "tornado emergency." The fifty-six thousand people of Moore, Oklahoma, had sixteen minutes to get to a safe place.

What did some residents of Moore do in sixteen minutes?

Patrick Smith grabbed his two kids from school, raced home, and jumped into the bathtub. He pulled a mattress over their heads.

Tracy Stephen rushed to school to get her six-year-old daughter, Abigail. The school doors were locked. With only a few minutes left, she climbed into the cellar of a neighbor's house with her two younger daughters. Her own home was wiped out by the storm. Later, she found Abigail alive. A teacher's aide had kept her safe when the school walls collapsed.

Carrie Long lost her home. Her two teenagers rode out the storm inside their classrooms.

How bad was the tornado that hit Moore?

The twister left more than a mile of destruction in its path. The storm rated a Category 5, as high as it goes.

THE AVERAGE WARNING TIMES IN THE U.S. FOR DEADLY STORMS ARE:

- Hurricane: 36 hours
- Flash floods: 64 minutes
- Severe thunderstorms: 18 minutes
- Tornadoes: 14 minutes

THE U.S. HAD NINE HUNDRED AND THIRTY-NINE TWISTERS IN 2012.

CAUSING ABOUT $7 BILLION IN DAMAGE.

What's a dust devil?

It's a tornado over a desert. When air rises over hot sand, it can start to spin like a tornado. Sometimes, these dust storms can reach a mile high and have wind speeds of 60 mph.

TRUTH or MYTH?

Tornadoes can only form over land.

MYTH! A tornado over a lake or sea is called a waterspout. Sometimes it's powerful enough to lift a boat out of the water!

Glossary

atmosphere—the layer of gases that surround the earth

bison—a large, hairy, grass-eating animal with a big head and short horns

buoyancy—the ability to float in water

compartment—a separate room or section

contamination—a state of being harmful or unclean

crater – a large round hole in the peak of a volcano

crude—in its natural state

custom—a habit or usual way of doing things

drought—a long period of little or no rain

epicenter—point on the earth's surface that is directly above the place where an earthquake starts

evacuate—to remove residents from a city or area for reasons of safety

fertile—capable of producing crops or offspring

habitat—the natural home of living plants or animals

iceberg—a large block of ice floating in the ocean

immigrant—a person who comes into a foreign country to live there

immune—protected from a disease, usually by inoculation

inoculate—to give a person a weak form of a disease in order to prevent infection by that disease

lava—magma, or molten rock, that reaches the earth's surface

levee—an embankment that is built to prevent water from flooding

magma—mass of molten rock deep below the earth's surface

migrant—a person who goes from one place to another, usually to find work

monsoon—the seasonal wind of the Indian Ocean that brings heavy rains to southern Asia

nuclear power—the high energy created by splitting apart the atoms of certain elements

organism—an individual living animal or plant

pandemic—an outbreak of a disease that spreads quickly to a large number of people over a wide area

plate—one of the large, slow-moving sections that make up the earth's surface

population—the total number of people living in an area

predator—an animal that hunts another animal for food

radar—a device that uses radio waves to find the position and speed of moving objects

radioactive—capable of sending out powerful rays caused when atoms are split apart

reactor—a large device that produces nuclear energy

Richter scale—a system for measuring the force of an earthquake or the energy it releases

saturated—completely filled with something

submersible—a ship that can operate underwater

surge—a sudden, forward movement

symbol—something used in place of something else

tenement—an apartment house, especially one in poorer, crowded parts of a city

tremor—a vibration or shaking of the ground

union—an organization of workers formed to protect their rights and interests